SWEET MACHINE

ALSO BY MARK DOTY

Turtle, Swan (1987)

Bethlehem in Broad Daylight (1991)

My Alexandria (1993)

Atlantis (1995)

Heaven's Coast (1996)

SWEET MACHINE

Poems

Mark Doty

HarperPerennial
An Imprint of HarperCollins*Publishers*

A HarperFlamingo edition of this book was published in 1998.

HarperCollins books may be purchased for educational, business, or sales promotional use. For information please write: Special Markets Department, HarperCollins Publishers, Inc., 10 East 53rd Street, New York, NY 10022.

First HarperPerennial edition published 1999.

Designed by Elina D. Nudelman

Library of Congress Cataloging-in-Publication Data

Doty, Mark.
Sweet Machine: poems / Mark Doty. — 1st ed.
p.   cm.
ISBN 0-06-055370-7 / ISBN 0-06-095256-3 (pbk.)
I. Title.
PS3554.0798S9   1998
811'.54—dc21   97-33215

01 02 HAD 10 9 8 7

Thou canst read nothing except through appetite . . .

—Hart Crane

ACKNOWLEDGMENTS

Grateful acknowledgments to the following publications, in which these poems appeared previously, often in earlier versions: *The Atlantic Monthly*: "The Embrace"; *Boulevard*: "Door to the River," "Messiah (Christmas Portions)"; *The Cimarron Review*: "White Kimono"; *Columbia*: "Fog Suite"; *Doubletake*: "One of the Rooming Houses of Heaven," "Sweet Machine"; *Green Mountains Review*: "Metro North"; *The Iowa Review*: "White Pouring"; *The Paris Review*: "Visitation"; *Ploughshares*: "Mercy on Broadway"; *PN Review*: "Retrievers in Translation"; *Poetry Review*: "Lilies in New York"; *Provincetown Arts*: "Emerald"; *Salon*: "Shelter"; *Sonora Review*: "Lilacs in NYC," "Murano"; *Southwest Review*: "Thirty Delft Tiles"; *Western Humanities Review*: "Favrile"; *The Yale Review*: "Where You Are."

"Golden Retrievals" appeared in *Unleashed* (Crown, 1996); "One of the Rooming Houses of Heaven" appeared in *Things Shaped in Passing: More Poets for Life Writing from the AIDS Pandemic* (Persea, 1996). "White Kimono" appeared as a chapbook published by the Instar Press, Tuscaloosa, Alabama; "Favrile" appeared in a limited edition volume published by the Dim Gray Bar Press, New York.

I'm grateful to the Mrs. Giles R. Whiting Foundation, the John Simon Guggenheim Foundation, the National Endowment for the Arts, and the Rockefeller Foundation's Bellagio Study Center for support which made the writing of these poems possible.

And to Paul: this book.

CONTENTS

FAVRILE

Glassmakers,
at century's end,
compounded metallic lusters

in reference
to natural sheens (dragonfly
and beetle wings,

marbled light on kerosene)
and invented names
as coolly lustrous

as their products'
scarab-gleam: *Quetzal,
Aurene, Favrile.*

Suggesting,
respectively, the glaze
of feathers,

that sun-shot fog
of which halos
are composed,

and—what?
What to make of *Favrile,*
Tiffany's term

for his coppery-rose
flushed with gold
like the alchemized

atmosphere of sunbeams
in a Flemish room?
Faux Moorish,

fake Japanese,
his lamps illumine
chiefly themselves,

copying waterlilies'
bronzy stems,
wisteria or trout scales;

surfaces burnished
like a tidal stream
on which an excitation

of minnows boils
and blooms, artifice
made to show us

the lavish wardrobe
of things, the world's
glaze of appearances

worked into the thin
and gleaming stuff
of craft. A story:

at the puppet opera
—where one man animated
the entire cast

while another ghosted
the voices, basso
to coloratura—Jimmy wept

at the world of tiny gestures,
forgot, he said,
these were puppets,

forgot these wire
and plaster fabrications
were actors at all,

since their pretense
allowed the passions
released to be—

well, operatic.
It's too much,
to be expected to believe;

art's a mercuried sheen
in which we may discern,
because it *is* surface,

clear or vague
suggestions of our depths.
Don't we need a word

for the luster
of things which insist
on the fact they're made,

which announce
their maker's bravura?
Favrile, I'd propose,

for the perfect lamp,
too dim and strange
to help us read.

For the kimono woven,
dipped in dyes, unraveled
and loomed again

that the pattern might take on
a subtler shading.
For the sonnet's

blown-glass sateen,
for bel canto,
for Fabergé.

For everything
which begins in limit
(where else might our work

begin?) and ends in grace,
or at least extravagance.
For the silk sleeves

of the puppet queen,
held at a ravishing angle
over her puppet lover slain,

for her lush vowels
mouthed by the plain man
hunched behind the stage.

White Kimono

Sleeves of oyster, smoke and pearl,
linings patterned with chrysanthemum flurries,
rippled fields: the import store's

received a shipment of old robes,
cleaned but neither pressed nor sorted,
and the owner's cut the bindings

so the bales of crumpled silks
swell and breathe. It's raining out, off-season,
nearly everything closed,

so Lynda and I spend an hour
overcome by wrinkly luxuries we'd never wear,
even if we could: clouds of—

are they plum blossoms?—
billowing on mauve, thunderheads
of pine mounting a stony slope,

tousled fields of embroidery
in twenty shades of jade:
costumes for some Japanese

midsummer's eve. And there,
against the back wall, a garment
which seems itself an artifact

of dream: tiny gossamer sleeves
like moth wings worrying a midnight lamp,
translucent silk so delicate

it might shatter at the weight
of a breath or glance.
The mere idea of a robe,

a slip of a thing
(even a small shoulder
might rip it apart)

which seems to tremble a little,
in the humid air. The owner—
enjoying our pleasure, this slow afternoon,

in the lush tumble of his wares—
gives us a deal. A struggle, to narrow it
to three: deep blue for Lynda,

lined with a secretive orange splendor
of flowers; a long scholarly gray for me,
severe, slightly pearly, meditative;

a rough raw silk for Wally,
its slubbed green the color of day-old grass
wet against lawn-mower blades. Home,

we iron till the kitchen steams,
revealing drape and luster.
Wally comes out and sits with us, too,

though he's already tired all the time,
and the three of us fog up the rainy windows,
talking, ironing, imagining mulberry acres

spun to this unlikely filament
—nearly animate stuff—and the endless
labor of unwinding the cocoons.

What strength and subtlety in these hues.
Doesn't rain make a memory more intimate?
We're pleased with our own calm privacy,

our part in the work of restoration,
that kitchen's achieved, common warmth,
the time-out-of-time sheen

of happiness to it, unmistakable
as the surface of those silks. And
all the while that fluttering spirit

of a kimono hung in the shop
like a lunar token, something
the ghost of a moth might have worn,

stirring on its hanger whenever
the door was opened—petal, phantom,
little milky flame lifting

like a curtain in the wind
—which even Lynda, slight as she was,
did not dare to try on.

WHERE YOU ARE

1.

flung to your salt parameters   in all that wide gleam
unbounded edgeless   in that brilliant intersection

where we poured   the shattered grit the salt
and distillation of you   which blew back

into my face stinging   like a kiss
from the other world   a whole year

you've languished blue   in ceaseless wind
naked now in all lights   and chill swaddlings

of cloud never for a moment   cold you are
uninterruptible seamless   as if all this time

you'd been sleeping   in the sparkle and beckon
of it are you   in the pour of it

as if there were a secret   shining room
in the house and you'd   merely gone there

we used to swim   summers remember
naked in those shoals   now I think was I ever

that easy   in this life
fireworks remember   Handel an orchestra

on a barge   in the harbor and fountains
spun to darkness   flung in time to

the music scrawling heaven   like sperm like
chrysanthemums bursting   in an enormous hurry

all fire and chatter   flintspark and dazzle
and utterly gone   save here in the scribble

of winter sunlight   on sheer mercury
when I was a child   some green Fourth

flares fretting   the blue-black night
a twirling bit of ash   fell in my open eye

and for a while I couldn't see   those skyrockets
is it like that now love   some cinder

blocking my sight   so that I can't see you
who are only for an hour   asleep and dreaming

in this blue   and light-shot room
as if I could lean across   this shifting watery bed

and ask   are you awake

2. EVERYWHERE

I thought I'd lost you. But you said *I'm imbued*

in the fabric of things, the way
that wax lost from batik shapes

the pattern where the dye won't take.
I make the space around you,

and so allow you shape. And always
you'll feel the traces of that wax
soaked far into the weave:
the air around your gestures,

the silence after you speak.
That's me, that slight wind between
your hand and what you're reaching for;
chair and paper, book or cup:

that close, where I am: between
where breath ends, air starts.

3. VAN GOGH, *Flowering Rosebushes*: 1889

A billow of attention
enters the undulant green,
and so configures it
to an unbroken rhythm,

summer's continuous surface,
dappled and unhurried
—though subject to excitations,
little swarms of shifting strokes

which organize themselves
into shadow and leaf, white starbursts

of bloom: a calm frenzy
of roses. His June's one green

unbordered sea, and he's gone
into it entirely—nothing here
but the confident stipple
and accumulation of fresh

and certain gesture, new again
in a rush of arrival. Don't you want
to be wrapped, brocaded,
nothing to interrupt

the whole struck field
in the various and singular
complexity of its music?
To be of a piece with the world,

whole cloth? These little passages
accrue, differ, bursts of white roses,
ripples and striations; what's Van Gogh
but a point of view? Missing

from the frame, he's everywhere,
though it would be wrong
to think him at the center
of the scene: his body's gone,

like yours. Rather it's as if
this incandescent stuff—
a wildly mottled Persian scarf
whose summery pattern

encapsulates shoreline and garden,
June's jade balconies of wave
and blossom tiered, one above the other,
in terraces of bloom—

were wrapped around him,
some splendid light-soaked silk,
weightless, motile, endlessly figured
and refiguring: gone into the paint,

dear, gone entirely into (*white rose*
& leaf, starry grasses) these waves
of arriving roses, the tumbling rose
of each arriving wave.

Lilies in New York

A drawing: smudged shadow, deep worked areas of graphite ren-
dering exactly a paper-wrapped pot's particular folds, then each
spiculate leaf, their complex spiraling movement up the stem,
and the shining black nodes—seeds?—mounted at the intersec-
tion of stalk and leaf: a work of attention all the way up to the
merest suggestion of the three flowers,
a few rough unmodulated lines . . .

what's this about? Why,

up here where trumpeting
crowns all this darkness,
has the artist given up?

Exhaustion, since he's made such
a density of strokes below?
This page moves from deep,

pressured rendering
toward these slight gestures,
the flower merely sketched,

barely represented. Is it that
he wants us to think, *This is a drawing,*
not a flower and so reminds us

that the power of his illusion,
alive below the lily's neck,
is trickery? A formal joke,

airy fragility over such a field of marks,
warring masses, particulate suspensions
(lead, black chalk, charred—coal?

smoothed or scribbled or crosshatched everywhere,
a made night): art's dialectic, the done
and undone, dirty worked spaces

and the clean blank gaze of the unfinished,
with all its airy invitations? Or is it
too much for him, to render that delicacy,

to bring the white throat out
of white paper, no hope of accuracy,
and so he makes this humble gesture

to acknowledge his own limitations,
because the lilies are perfect,
is that it, and what version

of their splendor would come any closer
than this wavering, errant line?
Or is he indifferent to flowering,

to culmination and resolution?
Would he rather remain with the push
of areas of darkness, hustle

and dash of line, cacophony of pot
and stem, roiling swoops and scrawls
like clashing swathes of twilight,

furious? As if the frame
were filled with colliding expanses
of noise (traffic, sirens, some engine

hammering into the street below,
barking, air brakes expelling their huge
mechanical tribute to longing,

arc of a train's passage and descent
below the river), as if charcoal
were a medium of solidified sound,

is that it, which allowed the grind
and pull of this city to render itself,
to pour through his hand

into its own representation
—which does not hobble our apprehension
of the thing but honors it, since it is

of the moment only, a singular
clarity, and we understand, don't we,
that stasis is always a lie?

These only appear to be lilies,
this conflation of smudges,
but isn't the ruse lovely,

matter got up in costume as itself?
Isn't the dark carved now,
a moment, around the body

of the flower? New York's
a clutch in which these lilies
are held, let's say the drawing's

subject is Manhattan's grip,
the instant in which the city
constellates itself

around this vertical stroke
risen from a blur of florist's paper:
doesn't all of New York lean

into the hard black lines defining
stalk and leaf, a field of pressure
and distortion, a storm

billowing and forming itself
now around these shapes?
Isn't the city flower and collision?

Trumpet, trumpet, and trumpet:
now New York's a smear
and chaos of lilies, a seized whir,

burr and diminishment, a greased dark
clank of lilies which contains in itself
snowy throat and black crosshatched

field of atmosphere, scent
and explosion, tenderness
and history, all that's leaning

down into the delicate, nearly human skin,
pressing with its impossible weight,
despite which the mouth of the flower

—quick and temporary as
any gesture made by desire—
remains open. Lustrous,

blackening, open as if
about to speak. Open—
is that it? Out of these negotiations

arises a sketchy, possible
bloom, about to, going to,
going to be, becoming

open. And who could hope to draw that?

Fog Suite

1. A FIVE-PANELED SCREEN

Fog-lacquered,
varnished in thin
pearl glaze,

the high dunes unfold,
a smudged sketch
for a folding screen,

panels inlaid
with cloudy ivory,
irregular patches

of grassy jade.
(The wide bay's
oddly still this morning,

despite the white activity
at its edges; just beyond the shore's
a huge, silvered equipoise.)

The fog is thinking
of burning away,
but for now

damp scarves
(unhemmed, like petals
of a white peony)

slide and tear
across this portion
of sky, sheets

of smudged paper
hung from heaven.
Trope on trope!

What I'm trying to do
is fix this impossible
shift and flux, and say

how this fog-fired
green's intensified
by sunlight filtered

through the atmosphere's
wet linens—a green
you could almost drink!

No trick of light
I'm talking about
but defiant otherness:

this sky's all
gorgeous trouble,
rain beginning

to fold the screen away.
Do we love more
what we can't say?

As if what we wanted
were to be brought
that much closer

to words' failure,
where desire begins?

2.

What I love about language
is what I love about fog:
what comes between us and things
grants them their shine. Take,

for instance, this estuary,
raised to a higher power
by airy sun-struck voile:
gunmetal cove and glittered bar

hung on the rim of the sky
like palaces in Tibet—
white buildings unreachable,
dreamed and held

at just that perfect distance:
the world's lustered by the veil.

3.
Or else I love fog
because it shows the world

as page, where much
has been written, and much erased.

Clapboards lose their boundaries,
and phantoms of summer's roses

loom like parade floats lost at sea.
Is that what it is,

visible uncertainty?
This evening the thin fact of it

appears a little at a time,
shawling streetlamps,

veiling the heights:
clocktower and steeple gone

in roiling insubstantiality.
I take fog as evidence,

a demonstration of the nothing
(or the nothing much)

that holds the world in place
—rehearsal for our roles

as billow and shroud, drift
and cloud and vanishing act?

And, between these figuring lines,
white space, without which

who could read? Every poem's
half erased. I'm not afraid;

it feels like home here,
held—like any line of text—

by the white margins
of a ghost's embrace.

Messiah (Christmas Portions)

A little heat caught
in gleaming rags,
in shrouds of veil,
    torn and sun-shot swaddlings:

over the Methodist roof,
two clouds propose a Zion
of their own, blazing
    (colors of tarnish on copper)

against the steely close
of a coastal afternoon, December,
while under the steeple
    the Choral Society

prepares to perform
Messiah, pouring, in their best
blacks and whites, onto the raked stage.
    Not steep, really,

but from here,
the first pew, they're a looming
cloudbank of familiar angels:
    that neighbor who

fights operatically
with her girlfriend, for one,
and the friendly bearded clerk
    from the post office

—tenor trapped
in the body of a baritone? Altos
from the A&P, soprano
   from the T-shirt shop:

   today they're all poise,
costume and purpose
conveying the right note
   of distance and formality.

   Silence in the hall,
anticipatory, as if we're all
about to open a gift we're not sure
   we'll like;

   how could they
compete with sunset's burnished
oratorio? Thoughts which vanish,
   when the violins begin.

   Who'd have thought
they'd be so good? *Every valley,*
proclaims the solo tenor,
   (a sleek blonde

   I've seen somewhere before
—the liquor store?) *shall be exalted,*
and in his handsome mouth the word
   is lifted and opened

into more syllables
than we could count, central *ab*
dilated in a baroque melisma,
   liquefied; the pour

of voice seems
to *make* the unplaned landscape
the text predicts the Lord
   will heighten and tame.

This music
demonstrates what it claims:
glory shall be revealed. If art's
   acceptable evidence,

mustn't what lies
behind the world be at least
as beautiful as the human voice?
   The tenors lack confidence,

and the soloists,
half of them anyway, don't
have the strength to found
   the mighty kingdoms

these passages propose
—but the chorus, all together,
equals my burning clouds,
   and seems itself to burn,

commingled powers
deeded to a larger, centering claim.
These aren't anyone we know;
   choiring dissolves

   familiarity in an up-
pouring rush which will not
rest, will not, for a moment,
   be still.

   Aren't we enlarged
by the scale of what we're able
to desire? Everything,
   the choir insists,

   might flame;
inside these wrappings
burns another, brighter life,
   quickened, now,

   by song: hear how
it cascades, in overlapping,
lapidary waves of praise? Still time.
   Still time to change.

DICKEYVILLE GROTTO

*The priest never used blueprints, but worked all
the many designs out of his head.*

Father Wilerus,
transplanted Alsatian,
built around
this plain Wisconsin

redbrick church
a coral-reef en-
crustation—meant,
the brochure says,

to glorify America
and heaven simul-
taneously. Thus:
Mary and Columbus

and the Sacred Heart
equally enthroned
in a fantasia of quartz
and seashells, broken

dishes, stalactites
and stick-shift knobs—
no separation
of nature and art

for Father Wilerus!
He's built fabulous blooms
—bristling mosaic tiles
bunched into chipped,

permanent roses—
and more glisteny stuff
than I can catalogue,
which seems to be the point:

a spectacle, saints
and Stars and Stripes
billowing in hillocks
of concrete. Stubborn

insistence on rendering
invisibles solid. What's
more frankly actual
than cement? Surfaced,

here, in pure decor:
even the railings
curlicued with rows
of identical whelks,

even the lampposts
and birdhouses,
and big encrusted urns
wagging with lunar flowers!

A little dizzy,
the world he's made,
and completely
unapologetic, high

on a hill in Dickeyville
so the wind whips
around like crazy.
A bit pigheaded,

yet full of love
for glitter *qua* glitter,
sheer materiality;
a bit foolhardy

and yet—sly sparkle—
he's made matter giddy.
Exactly what he wanted,
I'd guess: the very stones

gone lacy and beaded,
an airy intricacy
of froth and glimmer.
For God? Country?

Lucky man:
his purpose pales
beside the fizzy,
weightless fact of rock.

CONCERNING SOME RECENT CRITICISM OF HIS WORK

—*Glaze and shimmer,*
luster and gleam;

can't he think of anything
but all that sheen?

—No such thing,
the queen said,
as too many sequins.

CONCERNING SOME RECENT CRITICISM
OF HIS WORK

—*Glaze and shimmer,*
luster and gleam . . .

—What else to do
with what you adore

but build a replica?
My model theater's

an opera of atmospheres:
morning's sun-shot fog

hurried off the stage,
tidal gestures,

twilight's pour:
these gorgeous and

limited elements
which constitute

a universe, or verse.
And if I love

my own coinage,
recombinant elements

(I know, *lacquer*
and *tumble* and *glow,*

burnished and *fired*

and *hazed*) it's because
what else Lord

to wear? Every sequin's
an act of praise.

These bright distillates
mirror the day's

glossed terms—
what's the world but shine

and seem? She'd sewn

the wildly lavish thing
herself, and wore

—forgive me!— shimmer. . . .

Metro North

Over the terminal,
   the arms and chest
      of the god

brightened by snow.
   Formerly mercury,
      formerly silver,

surface yellowed
   by atmospheric sulphurs,
      acid exhalations,

and now the shining
   thing's descendant.
      Obscure passages,

dim apertures:
   these clouded windows
      show a few faces

or some empty car's
   filmstrip of lit frames
      —remember them

from school,
   how they were supposed
      to teach us something?—

waxy light hurrying
   inches away from the phantom
      smudge of us, vague

in spattered glass. Then
   daylight's soft charcoal
      lusters stone walls

and we ascend to what
   passes for brightness,
      this February,

scumbled sky
   above graduated zones
      of decline:

dead rowhouses,
   charred windows'
      wet frames

around empty space,
   a few chipboard polemics
      nailed over the gaps,

speeches too long
   and obsessive for anyone
      on this train to read,

sealing the hollowed interiors
   —some of them grand once,
      you can tell by

the fillips of decoration,
  stone leaves, the frieze
    of sunflowers.

Desolate fields—open spaces,
  in a city where you
    can hardly turn around!—

seem to center
  on little flames,
    something always burning

in a barrel or can.
  As if to represent
    inextinguishable,

dogged persistence?
  Though whether what burns
    is will or rage or

harsh amalgam
  I couldn't say.
    But I can tell you this,

what I've seen that
  won my allegiance most,
    though it was also

the hallmark of our ruin,
  and quick as anything
    seen in transit:

where Manhattan ends
    in the narrowing
        geographical equivalent

of a sigh (asphalt,
    arc of trestle, dull-witted
        industrial tanks

and scaffoldings, ancient now,
    visited by no one)
        on the concrete

embankment just
    above the river,
        a sudden density

and concentration
    of trash, so much
        I couldn't pick out

any one thing
    from our rising track
        as it arced onto the bridge

over the fantastic
    accumulation of jetsam
        and contraband

strewn under
    the uncompromising
        vault of heaven.

An unbelievable mess,
   so heaped and scattered
      it seemed the core

of chaos itself—
   but no, the junk was arranged
      in rough aisles,

someone's intimate
   clutter and collection,
      no walls but still

a kind of apartment,
   and a fire ribboned out
      of a ruined stove,

and white plates
   were laid out
      on the table beside it.

White china! Something
   was moving, and
      —you understand

it takes longer to tell this
   than to see it, only
      a train window's worth

of actuality—
   I knew what moved
      was an arm,

the arm of the (man
    or woman?) in the center
        of that hapless welter

in layer upon layer
    of coats blankets scarves
        until the form

constituted one more
    gray unreadable;
        whoever

was lifting a hammer,
    and bringing it down
        again, tapping at

what work
    I couldn't say;
        whoever, under

the great exhausted dome
    of winter light,
        which the steep

and steel surfaces of the city
    made both more soft
        and more severe,

was making something,
    or repairing,
        was in the act

(sheer stubborn nerve of it)
   of putting together.
      Who knows what.

(And there was more,
   more I'd take all spring
      to see. I'd pick my seat

and set my paper down
   to study him again
      —*he*, yes, some days not

at home though usually
   in, huddled
      by the smoldering,

and when my eye wandered
   —five-second increments
      of apprehension—I saw

he had a dog!
   Who lay half in
      half out his doghouse

in the rain, golden head
   resting on splayed paws.
      He had a ruined car,

and heaps of clothes,
   and things to read—
      was no emblem,

in other words,
   but a citizen,
      who'd built a citizen's

household, even
   on the literal edge,
      while I watched

from my quick,
   high place, hurtling
      over his encampment

by the waters of Babylon.)
   Then we were gone,
      in the heat and draft

of our silver, rattling
   over the river
      into the South Bronx,

against whose greasy
   skyline rose that neoned
      billboard for cigarettes

which hostages
   my attention, always,
      as it is meant to do,

its motto ruby
   in the dark morning:
      ALIVE WITH PLEASURE.

One of the Rooming Houses of Heaven

Last night I dreamed of Bobby again,
my old friend dead these years.
Funny he's the one who comes
back to me; we weren't ever that close,

but sometimes I hear him talking
in the kitchen, while I'm cooking,
his disdain for whatever I'm dreaming up
almost affectionate. Last night

we were in a hotel between worlds,
the kind of place where he felt
most at home: good heat in the radiators,
easy rent, bath down the hall,

everything simple. We were lying around
on his narrow bed, something comfortable
about it, the green shade pulled
almost all the way down because

I wasn't supposed to see.
He was telling me—in his soft,
exasperated way, not too impressed
with anything, in confidence,

as though possessed of the best gossip
—about the other world,
what it's like, though of course
I can't remember now a single thing he said.

EMERALD

Bureaus angled like ziggurats,
round-mirrored vanities in African veneers:
today they're taking Franco's furniture away,

art deco stuff the auction workers haul
into a long van chrome as this severe
March afternoon, the clouds harshly pearled.

He's been dead two months, and his things
—shy, in daylight, self-consciously
moderne—can't help but call him back:

summer nights he'd come dashing out
in his tuxedo, practically leaping into
the flame of his little convertible, driving

the four blocks to his restaurant,
its motto unforgettable and just:
We don't do anything simply at Franco's.

From my kitchen window I'd see
his red kitchen glow, when he'd cook
for the handsome Quebecois boys

he loved. He closed the restaurant,
the last six months,
but restless, sanguine as his little car,

went right to work, converting
his apartment to a gallery
of zigzag *objets*, another era's

streamlined embodiments
of artifice—a style which doesn't,
so to speak, bother to color its roots.

He hammered and painted,
hung out signs—though the important part,
plainly, was not business

(these things too precious
and unlikely to sell) but pleasure.
The wooden sign was pink and gray.

The bronze nude—who used to make
a display of herself in the restaurant garden,
lithe, long-necked, arms flung straight

at heaven—moved to Franco's lawn,
and at Christmas someone hung a wreath
around her neck, which made her look chilly.

He had Pneumocystis again and again.
In January her bronze breasts seemed blue.
Is it true, that death makes a mockery

of style? In today's obituaries,
no surprise, the same grinding news:
here's another man I barely knew,

one who used to dance at the A-House,
the writer says, *in the seventies,*
with a tambourine, long red hair streaming,

and around his neck, always, his favorite
emerald. I've read that story again
and again: *He loved his collection*

of sparkling beads, no one could forget
the dinners he used to host under the trees. . . .
Death mock style? Think of Franco,

coughing in his gallery, not tired,
constructing his universe of display.
Beauty's also a matter of power,

a way to say, *Look, this I make.*
What's identity but a forged glamour?
Isn't it style that mocks death?

                              Listen, dears,
it's early yet, the moon not yet risen;
she's still smoking in her room,
considering the evening's attitude

and maquillage, what false
unreadable names to scrawl
on the harbor tonight.
Time to dress, loves, time to choose

your signatures: time for the flattering,
the revelatory, time to conceal,
time for the rhinestones, the wigs,
a little blush? Would you prefer

these leathers' polished gestures,
poses and trappings of severity?
Don't you miss desire? Phantoms,
it's yours, the summer evening perpetual:

time to go out, time to appear
beneath the warm lights' enchantments,
Time for shattered dock lights
on the waterfront's oily satin,

the dark opening to admit us.
How far could you go?
This town's endless, avenues
and bowers, shadowy piers inviting

a kiss or gestures less personal but
no less tender. Don't you miss longing?
This haunted town's unrolled
under a knowing moon: our accomplice,

benevolent jade, she's the only one
who won't be seduced. Come back
in your great and snaking chain,
come back scorched and whirling,

you handsome wraiths
unspooling yards of figured silk,
nameless now, countless, memory stitched
like some lavish oriental tattoo,

dragon of hurrying shades
attended by your retinues, surrounded
by your accoutrements—deco, emerald,
the radiant beads—

          with which you made
yourselves. *My* emerald, you understand,
this flashing thing I've made of you

—of him, of them. I thought I heard,
a little, murmurous voicings, laughter
across the water, hiss of fireworks

somewhere behind the flares.
But there aren't any skyrockets here,
just that bit of burning hung

in these high bare branches, a winter lantern
above these gray and boarded streets.

Town so empty, off season,
you'd think that everybody'd died.

MURANO

*Close my eyes and I'm a vessel. Make it
some lucent amphora, Venetian blue . . .*

—Lynda Hull

Toxic salts, arsenic and copper,
metal oxides firing the glassmaker's slag
to meteor lusters; sheet-glass

married to a hammered golden foil
then cut to bits: the gilt tiles
of the Byzantines—masters

brought to San Marco
to approximate, in jeweler's terms,
      heaven—

           were set
not flush but at subtle angles, askew,
so the basilica's least daylight flickered

back to ether,
             returned to Sender.
Broken, the better to glitter.

Was that your intention,
to break apart just enough
to shine? What's forged

without heat, or gleams without
a blush of poison?
                    Outside Palazzo Grassi

—Fiat owns it now—upturned floodlamps
fire beneath the Grand Canal, so that light

through the stirred and ceaseless Adriatic
scrawls on ocher walls a rippling
suspiration:
                    republic of instability,

in love
     with reflection, made,
          in its every aspect,

to give back light.
     To God?
          I don't think so.

Even the pigeons' sleek necks
prismed, and some backwater's slick
of engine oil swirls like endpapers

marbled in opulent inks: *marmora*,
rich marble veins, *il pavone*, peacock's tail
multiplied to a profusion we'd call

—what else?—Venetian;

when I learned
        the patterns' names,
            it was you I wanted to tell,

no matter you've become
        a set of atmospheres.
            To whom else

would I write,
        from these opiate islands,
            this ashen year?

There's a Cornell box,
        in the Palazzo Venier, his version
            of a Byzantine vitrine:

ranks of little bottles,
        sealed and rowed
            on shelves before

the doubling mercury
        of a shiny American mirror.
            (Not one of those foggy,

Venetian glasses; their mineral opacity
gives back, mostly, themselves—cloudy,
unlikely as their source. Is glass
this town's metaphor for itself?

Hallucinatory, fragile, dangerous:
distorting sulphurs and hazes,
dissolving palaces, molten appearances

on unstable ground.)
   Cornell's canopic jars
      preserve sands

and tinctures,
   volatile unguents,
      shreds of map and text.

One's a sealed vial
   of nothing
      but radiant gold;

only paint,
   treasure gathered
      in the dimestores

of Manhattan,
   but it doesn't matter;
      this work—this *city*—

lives for the glamour
   we make of whatever's
      here. What's gold

but a physical
   species of joy?
      Venice is a world

of things he—and you—would cherish:
a jeweler's window Byzantine with marcasite,
a chilly galaxy you'd have worn,

its glitter restrained by the intimate alley
where jewelry's all that torches the dark.
Here's a clutch of Tintoretto silks, the sort

a girl in his turbulent air might bend to lift
as she hurries past the dim doorway of a room
where some miracle or martyrdom's occurring.

Here's another century's twilight
seeping between the columns,
winged lion, conquering saint,

portals of the dawn and evening
(which is which? in the Republic,
day began at sundown, a detail

you'd have liked),
    glassy radiance
        suffusing shell-pink

on leaden domes,
    facades of blackened marble,
        streetlamps greening on.

I'd never have understood
    the Cornell, if I hadn't seen it
        in Venice: he's made

this city's reliquary,
    perfect jewel-case to hold
        an empire's knucklebone,

scraps of its fabrics
    and foils, its sour essences,
        precious vapors and perfumes:

capital of the made, dear,
    where the given's smoked
        and polished, plucked

from the ovens'
    chemical heats, beaten
        and gilded to glory:

rotting palaces flung straight
    up from the sea, yellow
        of mummy wrappings,

coral and rose
    moldering now, faded
        to precisely these

bruised and mottled
    rusts; acid, lichenous
        greens: vitriolized,

encrusted, pearled.
    The city of artifice,
        darling, the city I love,

is a nightmare.
   Doesn't it smell
      of piss and dissolution,

isn't it glazed
   with its own whispers,
      this tide-licked,

self-absorbed, indifferent
   place? These mirrors
      reflect themselves,

not you. Is this
   what becomes of art,
      the hard-won permanence

outside of time? A struck
   match-head of a city,
      ungodly lonely

in its patina of fumes
   and ash? Gorgeous scrap heap
      where no one lives,

or hardly anyone
Did you have to burn
so harshly bright?
Wasn't the world
ruin enough? Why
break yourself further
and faster?

This dock
rocks and pitches, no solid
place to stand, and
on the lagoon's surface
a red boat's flank is troubled
into jasper, foaming
furnace-sheen. A *vaporetto*

(hear, even in the word,
wild instability,
                    homage to mutable
airs and smokes?)
                    to Murano,

island of the glassmakers'
    exile. Wise city, to banish
        this business

to its margins,
    ancient ovens fired
        all millennium

to incandescence.
    Even a pouring, refracted city
        must protect itself.

Are you afraid,
    now you're salts and essences,
        the flung and gathered

elements from which any art
   is fused and blown?
      When were you ever

afraid to be spun out
   into some other order,
      alloyed with strange metals,

thinned, dosed
   with just enough
      to become radiant,

skin flushed with azure
   and a Pharaoh's wash of gold?
      Here the brilliant liquid

tormented into form,
   pincers and tongs,
      mouthpieces and pipes

to shape and set you
   spinning. Always
      the fate of the maker,

to become what's made
   —the gilt, permanent thing,
      of silk or sentences,

metal or silicas?
   Did I tell you I saw,
      on a dusty lower shelf

in the Treasury of San Marco,
   a pair of golden birds
      welded to a golden bough

complete with hammered leaves,
   some Grecian goldsmith's
      bright-beaked accomplishment

stolen from Byzantium?
                      And now you're glass.

Thirty Delft Tiles

Iconic, archetypal as tattoos, in lapis,
delphinium, bruise: a spread of cards,

the blue and white, promising tableaux
of some chipped porcelain tarot:

antique tiles, in a Stonington window,
November, all the stores closed,

dealers gone. This one,
a Mrs. Mahler, has left a number,

but she's not at home today,
when I'd love to inquire after

the mermaid on her outcrop of stone,
the cornflower rooster crowing

in his field of crackled glaze.
A boy pipes though blurry fields

on a blurred flute;
a rinsed hare leaps; a hero

raises to heaven his inky sword:
spirits of Water Street, these images, after

my visit with you. I couldn't bring myself
to call you Jimmy, though you asked.

We sat over coffee in your round red room.
You were gracious, playful and probably

thoroughly bored by me, stricken as I was
by shyness in the company of a Great Man.

The cup you raised (I liked how none
of the china on that round glass matched

or even bore relation) was Spode,
Blue Italian. I know because Yeats

favored the pattern, too, and once
I tried to read its skyey plot

in a case at Thoor Ballylee:
a pastoral opera lit entirely

in a single hue: gothic ruin,
country views unfolding

in exactly that 1950s
elementary-school-fountain-pen

blue. A laundress scrubs
by the riverbank. A priest reads.

Variable beasts
(a clutch of sheep, a cow or two)

stand up to their haunches
in the stream, number depending

on whether one studies the plate
or saucer, the platter or tureen.

Which is why, I imagine, you
and Yeats might like it: gestures

of surprise, inside the regularity
of form, hooved or human actors

playing out their parts beneath
the stippled trees, a fixed

but not quite scrutable tale
unified by this lavish ink.

Under your red room's dome,
we were assuming roles: the Elder

with his fairy charm—packed in ice
or salt?—the Pilgrim stiff and shy

and come to do honor. What we talked about,
I hardly recall: travel, poetry readings,

a local boy whose verse you'd been critiquing;
you were absolute grace, with that imperturbable

charm which both invites and protects,
manners aimed at holding the listener

just close enough. Sandy fixed your stereo
so you could play CDs. And then the tour,

which led to your apartment's secret core:
behind a hinged bookcase/door,

the book-paved room in which you wrote.
It felt like the interior of a heart.

Or one of those fancy evening purses,
a jeweled and beaded minaudière

turned inside out, the interior gemmed
with books, and centered on a draft

of rarest air. Out on the street again,
it seemed I'd breathed the dazzling

ozone of some other elevation.
That shop-window field of Delft

took on a decided tinge of you:
your cup's stenciled round

circling whatever it held at the core.
I called Mrs. Mahler for ages

before I finally found her home;
she quoted a price I couldn't afford.

Months later, a last view: on your gusty
terrace, a portrait bust:

one of the late Teutonic despots
of Rome, nose and haircut

given an Italian makeover
by the sculptor's sense of Caesarean

convention. Ditched by the local museum,
he's years enjoyed your harbor view,

but today three strong guys come to haul
the emperor away to a shady site

in Sandy's garden, a sheltered if less lofty
perch. Occasion for a tour, for Paul,

who's never seen the marvelous shell
of your apartment before: the paintings

and bric-a-brac of travel, and Sandover's
legendary props: bat wallpaper so dreadful

as to charm, the huge mirror your DJ hauled
upstairs, the circular chamber's bricky,

glowing rose, tin rotunda picked out
in painted detail—who was smoking what

when this place was decorated?
Furniture of a grand poem, these things

refresh by not being epic themselves:
unpretentious, warm still,

welling up with testimony of you.
Case in point: the Ouija board,

just a sheet of cardboard taped
and taped to that glass table till the corners

were nearly torn away. Beneath the arc
of alphabet, symbols you'd added,

for convenience' sake: &, some terms
the dead used often, and (unique to your

board in all the world) a slash mark,
so the spirits could indicate

a line break. We're in heaven, here among
your books, drafts of poems, evidence

of inhabitation so intense
it makes death seem—well, in-

consequential. Which you'd have liked,
I think—who ever so thoroughly

prepared his own afterlife?
Though nothing prepared *me*, quite,

for that willow-ware teacup,
your makeshift planchette

—nothing delicate but thick, and cracked,
and crazed with tea-stained lines where stress

had split the glaze, rough spots
where the cup was glued and dropped

and glued again: nothing you'd expect
to bear the tongues of angels,

but isn't that always the way?
God, my dear (is it too late to assume

the familiar now, as once you
asked me to?), is in the *damages*:

aren't we always, if we're lucky,
ruined into knowledge? Yet the cup's

lovers and bridges and birds
are cheerful and intact, antiphonal in azure

under their dime-store glaze.
Mrs. Mahler's sold the lot of Delft,

already installed in someone else's kitchen,
but what could it matter;

I'll be possessed *by* them,
a pack of tokens to shuffle and deal

like gypsy cards: Pilgrim, Hero, Sage,
no mere emblems but live

as the needled and figured skin
of some tough boy's lucky arms,

indigo and promising, the inky billows
of trees bent in this willow-ware glow.

There's no voice in the cup now, but
something like static, a crackle:

wind blowing off the crystal radio
of the stars? Those warm glowing tubes

inside the back of the night, is that
where the singing comes from?

Hear how they fill with it,
these willows risen at the rim,

their cobalt ruined,
furious and true.

The Embrace

You weren't well or really ill yet either;
just a little tired, your handsomeness
tinged by grief or anticipation, which brought
to your face a thoughtful, deepening grace.

I didn't for a moment doubt you were dead.
I knew that to be true still, even in the dream.
You'd been out— at work maybe?—
having a good day, almost energetic.

We seemed to be moving from some old house
where we'd lived, boxes everywhere, things
in disarray: that was the *story* of my dream,
but even asleep I was shocked out of narrative

by your face, the physical fact of your face:
inches from mine, smooth-shaven, loving, alert.
Why so difficult, remembering the actual look
of you? Without a photograph, without strain?

So when I saw your unguarded, reliable face,
your unmistakable gaze opening all the warmth
and clarity of you—warm brown tea—we held
each other for the time the dream allowed.

Bless you. You came back, so I could see you
once more, plainly, so I could rest against you
without thinking this happiness lessened anything,
without thinking you were alive again.

WHITE POURING

I was a swan,
and I slept in the reeds
by the highway,
by way of kind; ours,

pond's edge, always,
our narrow crescent
where liquid silver's
broken (both sky

and water pour)
by long strokes
of grasses. A chilly,
recalcitrant spring,

and oh, they were the world's
capital, the high wet plumes,
they were the morning
and evening fixed between

seed-littered heavens.
A swan's questions:
who feeds on the kindled
grains of the sky?

Whose feathers drifted
across the firmament
in a white highway
more steady than

your pouring hurry?
Our night place, still,
though the light-path
roars and headlamps fret

the tall grasses.
Unnumbered Aprils
—even if we counted
we could not measure—

we were held in
that sweet expanse, and bent
ourselves to form
on the waters symmetries

a swan doesn't need
or know, though I knew
in my long body,
from my heavy center

to the extravagance of neck
and the twin creakings
at either shoulder
—imagine wearing something

that opens furiously
out onto the world,
a body of opportunities
to touch . . .

Doubles for the wing
winter wrapped around us,
always. Then,
in the new months,

eggs shone in moonlight,
little domes rising
from the reedy nests,
versions of the vault

of heaven. It is not,
you understand,
in the nature of swans
to regret, but if it were

what I would miss
is the long unbroken
body of the dream,
giving ourselves

to it, how we were one
wing and water, one silver
unfurling from the white
womb-chamber of the shell

to pond to air's fierce music
to sleeping bent-necked
over the treasury of the future
again. . . .   But there, I speak

in human terms—
how else would you allow me
to frame the discussion?
We had no future,

simply the pour.
And now, in your sense,
we have no future again.
Not in our nature

to lament; I sleep here
in the chill shine
and am what I always was:
attention, a swirl of action

around a cluster of—terms,
really, at our common core:
hungry, white, eggs,
grass. Snow stays late,

the sky untunes
a harsher music.
Where are you hurrying,
in your cold metal?

The legend's passed.
Do you understand?
The beautiful kingdom is over.

RETRIEVERS IN TRANSLATION

The subject's always ostensible.
Here's a hunt, at the edge of a lake
—Como?—boys rushing into the water,
excited hounds swimming beside a stag

while one man throws his arms around
the antlered crown, a strange embrace
in the beast's last hour. By a reedy island
in the middle distance, boaters and paired swans

ignore the action, and the far shore recedes
into a romance of towers and tiny arches,
mountains flung into a haze of blue threads.
But it's not the grand prospect that matters;

what the weavers must have wanted to offer
is a universe of detail, lush field of incident
meant to warm a hall and fill the eye
with comic multiplicity. Comedy's the story

of other people, tragedy somehow always
about ourselves. Loss concentrates the gaze
to a singular focus, but the crowded world
says, *Here, look here*, and yields a confusion

of silk particulars. Odd, what bits emerge
as central: first the men's red buttocks
and calves, firm and jutting in their scarlet tights.
A sleeve's indigo billow, rope knotting a hunter's horn.

Intricate ivy. Then this pair of radiant details
steal the show: two dog faces, side by side,
retrievers—recognizable but, like Renaissance lions,
unmistakably Italian, as though they've been,

somehow, *translated*. One, blue-eyed,
is caught in profile, grinning, turned
to the action a dozen feet from shore;
the other looks directly at us, the textile hung

so that his eyes meet ours dead on
with a shocked—and shocking—immediacy:
animal eyes staring five hundred years
but new as the surprise of yellow primroses,

this morning, their low, steady candlepower
glowing the shade of villa walls in February rain.
Coral pupils center that buttery ivory,
parchment deepening to tones of varnish

and ocher, shellac and bronze,
alive with subdued heat. The life
of animals, the life of art;
they seem to meet in this gaze

which *is* fabric but looks back at us,
from the cinquecento and from the abyss
between dogs and people, beast to—
well, no one's this animal's master.

Just last week, in a classroom,
someone said to me, *What do you think
otherness is?* Here, almost palpable,
in the hall's cool glamour, hangs

a life which is not our life, intractable,
fixed, staring out, more alive than
the men who're sealed, with their bulging legs
and horned shoes, in the hunt's sphere

of fixed attention. They're lost to us,
but this dog's here, now, and made
to startle us to witness, mute friend
who invites us to speak for him, to him

—imagine the warm mellowed tongue,
the paw's solid heft—to reach a hand
toward these threads, the woven wools
and silks of text: *Good dog, bravo, come.*

GOLDEN RETRIEVALS

Fetch? Balls and sticks capture my attention
seconds at a time. Catch? I don't think so.
Bunny, tumbling leaf, a squirrel who's—oh
joy—actually scared. Sniff the wind, then

I'm off again: muck, pond, ditch, residue
of any thrillingly dead thing. And you?
Either you're sunk in the past, half our walk,
thinking of what you never can bring back,

or else you're off in some fog concerning
—tomorrow, is that what you call it? My work:
to unsnare time's warp (and woof!), retrieving,
my haze-headed friend, you. This shining bark,

a Zen master's bronzy gong, calls you here,
entirely, now: bow-wow, bow-wow, bow-wow.

SHELTER

They shove
 and tumble around us
  on the concrete floor,

the little ones,
 just as they must have crowded
  around the gates of this world,

eager to live. So much
 to be licked, on earth,
  what work! All mouth, sure

of their reception,
 they've hurried to a realm
  they know will feed them,

so they open their new faces
 to us, tongues and teeth
  apprehending our scents

and salts. *This is here,*
 the minds register, *yes,*
  and this, and this is good.

The older ones, each
 in a separate pen, consider
  what's to be made

of betrayal. This one's
　　all evident eagerness,
　　　　muzzle against the grid;

this one serenely still,
　　waiting for us to make
　　　　the first gesture, though

there's something—hopeful?—
　　in his expression. The one
　　　　who's been here longest

cries, though not to us.
　　Rowed under
　　　　the hellgate inscriptions

(*Too big, No time,*
　　Landlord says no)
　　　　they've lost habitations

and, some of them, names,
　　though most carry forward
　　　　a single word—

Tahoe, Dakota, Jack—
　　all of the past they're allowed
　　　　to keep, and not enough

to stop the world from draining
　　into this vague limbo
　　　　far from affection's locations

and routines. I know.
    Leashed to no one,
        the plain daily habits

gone, who are we?
    No one's dog
        is nothing but eagerness

tempered with caution,
    though only a little.
        We wanted to be born

once, don't we want
    to be delivered again,
        even knowing the nothing

love may come to?
    O Lucky and Buddy and Red,
        we put our tongues to the world.

DOOR TO THE RIVER

—de Kooning

He means, I think, there's an out,

built of these fistfuls of yellows.
Means, I think, there's a door,

in this passionate and hard-won
approximation, in this rough push

and lemon smear, this difficulty,

there's—what? In the meadows,
yesterday, great heavy presences

of the trees thinking, rimmed

around the perimeter of the field:
pendulous, weighted, trees

here to be emerald pull
and resistance, suspended

their given hour, the meadow arranging itself

into this huge composition which invites
and resists at once, the world's hung

surface: aren't we always wanting
to push beyond it, as if behind the scrim

—old lure and spur, old promise—

lay . . . The bright core
breathing? Why can't you just

love sheer play, these forms'
dynamic irresolutions

on the surface of the day?

These trees only seem still,
fixed their hour in the rush

and suction from that gate:
can't you just walk between the yellow

word *field* and the green word *door*
and not demand to penetrate

the primed and stubborn scrim
toward some clarity beyond forms?

Written in a sidewalk's new cement:
Be happy it's really all you have.

Happiness? Our possession
is yellow and green, dialectic

occupying the meadows,

arranging for us this moment
and the next (I'm not afraid

to die, I'm afraid to continue
in this tumult of collisions

and vanishing),
                    the ocher word
meadow, the green word *door*.
                              Listen,

there's a door in these yellow handfuls,
these wild strokes.
                    Haven't you walked

into something like happiness but larger?
Just yesterday, inside the meadow's

goldenrod perimeter,
near evening, in the stubble-grass,

eye-level with furled umbels
of wild carrot, chains of burr

and burdock and the clovers' half-dry blooms,

I pressed my stomach against
the warm surface of the field,

sunlight drowsing and slanting
toward us while the dogs and I

lay easy and with no need to be
anywhere. We heard a woman calling,

in a European accent, German maybe, her dog,

her chocolate Lab, who was mousing
with great patience and dedication, and she

with her patience and dedication
was calling *Jackie, Jackie* without urgency

because she knew that Jackie would come.

That's when I went through
the door. It was her voice,

the name pronounced softly
over and over above the tender

yellow scent of the grass and the hurry

of intimately related and endlessly
varied yellows, the sunflowers'

golden insistences, little violet
spikings in the eyes of the asters

sparking the whole field into something

like a quivering although entirely still,
and still my two curled companions

not sleeping but like me

alert and perhaps also poised
at an instant when the whole ceaseless

push and tumble arrived at some
balance and there was no lack, nothing

missing from the world,
and for the duration of that sheen

—during which you know
this moment of equipoise

is one more movement of light

and flesh and grass passing through
the corridor, the world's wild maw

of dynamic motion—
Jackie, she said, *Jackie*, yellow word,

and for that astonished instant

hung on the other side, permitted
entrance to the steep

core of things you think
of course this is what death

will be. Fine.

MY TATTOO

I thought I wanted to wear
the Sacred Heart, to represent
education through suffering,

how we're pierced to flame.
But when I cruised
the inkshop's dragons,

cobalt tigers and eagles
in billowy smokes,
my allegiance wavered.

Butch lexicon,
anchors and arrows,
a sailor's iconic charms—

tempting, but none
of them me. What noun
would you want

spoken on your skin
your whole life through?
I tried to picture what

I'd never want erased
and saw a fire-ring corona
of spiked rays,

flaring tongues
surrounding—an emptiness,
an open space?

I made my mind up.
I sat in the waiting room chair.
Then something (my nerve?

faith in the guy
with biker boots
and indigo hands?)

wavered. It wasn't fear;
nothing hurts like grief,
and I'm used to that.

His dreaming needle
was beside the point;
don't I already bear

the etched and flaring marks
of an inky trade?
What once was skin

has turned to something
made; written and revised
beneath these sleeves:

hearts and banners,
daggers and flowers and names.
I fled. Then I came back again;

isn't there always
a little more room
on the skin? It's too late

to be unwritten,
and I'm much too scrawled
to ever be erased.

Go ahead: prick and stipple
and ink me in:
I'll never be naked again.

From here on out,
I wear the sun,
albeit blue.

SWEET MACHINE

Glisten fretting the indigo of a plum,
silvered chalk of moth-wing dust:

the young man on the subway platform
—twenty maybe—seems almost powdered,

he is so dirty, the dust lighter
than his skin, which is still,

by a slight stretch of the imagination,
lovely. Though it's odd to think

of him that way, this shirtless kid
in hugely oversized jeans that fall,

when he stands, around his thighs,
exposing his skinny ass. He yanks

the waistband up, sits down again,
and begins to writhe, palms roaming,

uncontrollable, over his own face,
his close-cropped hair and ears,

down to his flanks, hands disappearing
inside the big jeans, scratching

and rubbing, until he collapses, exhausted,
head hanging between his knees,

and after a few seconds starts
it all up again. Does he want

to rub his own skin away? Then
I understand: what's powdering his flesh *is*

his flesh, the outest layer of himself
rubbed to palest chalk. He repeats

his stream of violent tableaux;
these might be positions of transport,

of ecstasy, except he's miserable, I guess,
and it's two in the afternoon, 96th and Broadway,

and all of us waiting for the local
watch, how can we help it? *Crackhead,*

somebody says, but it's a whisper, a question,
and nothing answers our troubled fascination:

nothing to do but watch the pity and terror
of these poses. The express comes and goes,

and the brutal series grows more synaptic:
these might be flashes of the pornographic,

or classical attitudes, rough trade posing
as a captive slave for Michelangelo. Our context's

neither intimate nor academic, and nothing's
supposed to be so real in the common nowhere

of the on-the-way-to, while we wait
for the 1 or the 9, strangers and witnesses

pressed knee to hem, back to shoulder
on the platforms and cars. This month,

on the broad haunches of the buses,
another sleek boy's posed in multiple shots,

black underwear and lean belly laved by rivulets
from a shower or stream. The photographer's

left him headless, his gestures multiplied
on builders' makeshift walls, page after page

of blank torsos already beginning to be inscribed:
on a yard of silvery muscle six feet from Seventh Avenue

someone's scrawled, in black marker: *I am a sweet
suck and fuck machine. Take me home.* Big buses

nose through the streets, one after the other,
bearing the model of what we're supposed to want,

and do, what we're meant to see and need
but not, unless we have the money, touch.

He doesn't have the money, my boy
on the platform, and I wish. . . . What?

I don't know. Just today, in traffic,
one of those buses eased by my taxi window:

a taut wet waist bound in black elastic,
huge, luminous emulsion inches

from my face. The endlessly reprinted boy
—is he?—could almost be *this* man,

whitened by his own degrading skin,
dark stone wearing the dust of the quarry.

He's rubbing himself to flour, he's giving
his name back to airy nothing, I'm figuring him

on the varnished bench. Moth, plum—hear
how the imagery aestheticizes? He's nothing

as fixed as marble, and he touches himself
not for pleasure but because he can't stop.

What unthinkable train is he waiting for?
That boy on the billboard, the headless boy,

could he stop touching himself?
We're all on display in this town,

sweet machines, powerless, consumed,
just as he consumes himself

with those relentless hands,
scratching his barely hidden center,

hanging his head between his knees,
spent, before he jerks himself up

and starts all over again.

Lilacs in NYC

Monday evening, E. 22nd
   in front of Jimmy and Vincent's,
a leafing maple, and it's as if

Manhattan existed in order
   to point to these
leaves, the urbane marvel

of them. Tuesday AM
   at the Korean market,
cut, bundled lilacs, in clear

or silvered cellophane—
   mist & inebriation,
cyclonic flames in tubs

of galvanized aluminum,
   all along Third Avenue,
as if from the hardy rootstocks

of these shops sprouted
   every leaf-shine and shade
of panicle: smoke, plum, lavender

like the sky over the Hudson,
   some spring evenings, held
in that intoxicating window

the horizontal avenues provide.
    Numbered avenues,
dumb beautiful ministers. . . . Later,

a whole row of white crabapples
    shivering in the wind
of a passing train; later,

a magnolia flaring
    in a scatter
of its own fallen petals,

towering out of a field
    of itself. Is that what
we do? I've felt like that,

straddling my lover,
    as if I rose
out of something

which resembled me,
    joined at the trunk
as if I come flaming

up out of what I am,
    the live foam muscling
beneath me. . . .

Strong bole thrust up
    into the billow,
into the frills and the insistences

and elaborations,
    the self flying open!
They're flowers, they know

to fall if they bloom;
    blessed relief of it,
not just myself this little while.

You enter me and we are strangers
    to ourselves but not
to each other, I enter you

(strange verb but what else
    to call it—to penetrate
to fuck to be inside of

none of the accounts of the body
    were ever really useful were they
tell the truth none of them),

I enter you (strange verb,
    as if we were each an enclosure
a shelter, imagine actually

considering yourself a *temple*)
    and violet the crush of shadows
that warm wrist that deep-hollowed

collar socket those salt-lustered
    lilacy shoulderblades,
in all odd shadings of green and dusk . . .

blooming in the field
   of our shatter. You enter me
and it's Macy's,

some available version of infinity;
   I enter you and I'm the grass,
covered with your shock

of petals out of which you rise
   Mr. April Mr. Splendor
climbing up with me

inside this rocking, lilac boat.
   My candlelight master,
who trembles me into smoke-violet,

as April does to lilac-wood.

MERCY ON BROADWAY

Saturday, Eighth and Broadway,
a dozen turtles the color of crushed mint

try for the ruby rim
of a white enamel bowl

on the sidewalk, wet jade
jewel cases climbing two

or three times the length
of their bodies toward heaven

till the slick sides of the bowl
send them sliding back into

their brothers' bright heap
of grassy armament. The avenue's

a high wall of what the clubs call
deep house mix: tribal rave

from the flea market across the street,
some deejay hawking forty-five-minute sides

of pure adrenaline, snarl and sputter
and staccato bass of traffic and some idling taxi,

siren wail's high arc over it all,
blocks away, and the call and response

of kids on both sides of the avenue,
some flashing ripple of Motown sparking

the whole exhaust-shimmered tapestry
like gold thread *don't forget*

the motor city and even some devotees'
hare rama droned in for good measure

in the sheer seamless scrim
of sound this town is, so at first

I can't make out the woman
beside me saying *You want buy turtle?*

I don't want any one of this
boiling bowl of coppery citizens

longing for release—a dozen maybe,
or nothing at all. So much to want

in this city, the world's bounty
laid out, what's the point in owning

any one piece of it? Deep house mix:
these hip-hop kids disappearing

into huge jackets and phat jeans,
these Latin girls with altarpiece earrings,

homo boys eyeing each other's big
visible auras of self-consciousness

all the way across Broadway,
vendors from Senegal Hong Kong

and Staten Island selling
incense sweatshirts peanuts

roasted in some burning sugar syrup.
What do you want right now?

What can't the city teach you
to want? It's body atop body here,

lovely and fragile armor dressed up
as tough, it's so many beats there's

something you can dance to, plan on it,
flash and hustle all up and down

this avenue. Don't let it fool you,
grief's going down all over

these blocks, invisible only
because indifferent and ravenous

Broadway swallows it all,
a blowsy appetite just as eager

to eat you as to let you go;
maybe you're someone in particular

but no offense pal no one's necessary
to the big sound of the avenue's

tribal, acid mix.
I'm standing here bent

over this bowl of turtles—
green as Asia, sharp-edged

as lemongrass—and ruthless
as I know this street is

nowhere, nowhere to run to,
nowhere to hide this morning there's no place

I'd rather be than smack in the thrall
of Broadway's merciless matter

and flash, pulse and trouble. *Turtle?*
You want? Their future can't be bright;

what's one live emerald clutch purse
in the confusion and glory

Manhattan is? Listen, I've seen fever
all over this town, no mercy, I've seen

the bodies I most adored turned to flame
and powder, my shattered darlings

a clutch of white petals lifted
on the avenue's hot wind:

last night's lottery tickets
crumpled chances blown in grates

and gutters. I'm forty-one years old
and ready to get down

on my knees to a kitchen bowl
full of live green. I'm breathing here,

a new man next to me who's beginning
to matter. *It's gonna take a miracle*

sings any one of the untraceable radios
or tape decks or personal hookups to the music

of the spheres threading this fluid
and enormous crowd *to make me love*

someone new. I don't think these turtles
are going to make it, but what

does that mean? Maybe an hour
on Broadway's jewel enough.

Unthinkably green now, they're inseparable
from the sudden constellation

of detail the avenue's become
—this boulevard continuously radiant,

if only we could see it—live integers
of this streaming town's

lush life. As you and I are, boy,
laughing and strolling and taking our parts

in its plain vulgar gorgeousness,
its cheap and shining aspirations.

I want what everybody wants,
that's how I know I'm still

breathing: deep mix, rapture
and longing. Let me take your arm,

in that shiny blue jacket I love,
clear plastic pendants hung

like bijoux from its many zippers,
let me stand close to you in the way

the avenue allows, let the sun flash
on your chrome ring, let me praise

your sideburns and your black baseball cap,
signifying gestures that prove

gonna take a miracle we're living.
I've been lucky; I've got a man

in my head who's spirit and ash
and flecks of bone now, and a live one

whose skin is inches from mine.
I've been granted this reprieve,

and I'll take whatever part
Broadway assigns me: Man on His Knees

Beside a Bowl of Turtles, Man on the Sidewalk
with His Heart in His Mouth? Let's walk,

let's drink this city street's
ash and attitude, scorch and glory,

its human waves of style and talk,
its hundred thousand ways to say

Hey. I looked into that shiny cup
of ambulant green and I thought

Somebody's going to live through this.
Suppose it's you? Whatever happens to me,

to us, somebody's going to ride out
these blasted years, somebody if I'm still lucky

years from now will read this poem and walk
on Broadway. Broadway's no one,

and Broadway lasts. Here's the new
hat, the silhouette of the summer. Here's

the new jewelry everybody's wearing,
the right haircut, the new dance, the new song,

the next step, the new way of walking, the world
that's on everyone's lips, the word that's on its way:

our miracle Broadway, our hour.

VISITATION

When I heard he had entered the harbor,
and circled the wharf for days,
I expected the worst: shallow water,

confusion, some accident to bring
the young humpback to grief.
Don't they depend on a compass

lodged in the salt-flooded folds
of the brain, some delicate
musical mechanism to navigate

their true course? How many ways,
in our century's late iron hours,
might we have led him to disaster?

That, in those days, was how
I'd come to see the world:
dark upon dark, any sense

of spirit an embattled flame
sparked against wind-driven rain
till pain snuffed it out. I thought,

This is what experience gives us,
and I moved carefully through my life
while I waited. . . .   Enough,

it wasn't that way at all. The whale
—exuberant, proud maybe, playful,
like the early music of Beethoven—

cruised the footings for smelts
clustered near the pylons
in mercury flocks. He

(do I have the gender right?)
would negotiate the rusty hulls
of the Portuguese fishing boats

—Holy Infant, Little Marie—
with what could only be read
as pleasure, coming close

then diving, trailing on the surface
big spreading circles
until he'd breach, thrilling us

with the release of pressured breath,
and the bulk of his sleek young head
—a wet black leather sofa

already barnacled with ghostly lice—
and his elegant and unlikely mouth,
and the marvelous afterthought of the flukes,

and the way his broad flippers
resembled a pair of clownish gloves
or puppet hands, looming greenish white

beneath the bay's clouded sheen.
When he had consumed his pleasure
of the shimmering swarm, his pleasure, perhaps,

in his own admired performance,
he swam out the harbor mouth,
into the Atlantic. And though grief

has seemed to me itself a dim,
salt suspension in which I've moved,
blind thing, day by day,

through the wreckage, barely aware
of what I stumbled toward, even I
couldn't help but look

at the way this immense figure
graces the dark medium,
and shines so: heaviness

which is no burden to itself.
What did you think, that joy
was some slight thing?

NOTES

"White Kimono" remembers Lynda Hull, 1954–1994, and Wally Roberts, 1951–1994.

"Lilies in New York," for Jorie Graham, is titled after a drawing by Jim Dine.

The epigraph to "Dickeyville Grotto" is drawn from a brochure published by the Dickeyville Grotto Association, Dickeyville, Wisconsin.

"One of the Rooming Houses of Heaven" is for Robert Shore, 1948–1993.

The epigraph to "Murano" is from Lynda Hull's "Rivers into Seas," from *The Only World*.

"Thirty Delft Tiles" is for James Merrill, 1926–1995.

"White Pouring" is for Maggie Valentine.

The tapestry in "Retrievers in Translation" hangs in the Villa Serbelloni, Bellagio, Italy.

"Golden Retrievals," for Robert Jones, is spoken by Beau.

"Shelter" is for Michael Carter.

"Door to the River" is titled after Willem de Kooning's 1960 painting in the collection of the Whitney Museum of American Art.

"Lilacs in NYC" owes the notion of the department store as an "available version of infinity" to an essay by Eric Zencey, "Xeno's Mall," from his book *Virgin Forest*.

"Mercy on Broadway" is titled after a song by the late Laura Nyro.

About the Author

MARK DOTY is the author of four poetry collections and the memoir *Heaven's Coast*, which won the PEN/Martha Albrand Award for First Nonfiction. He is the recipient of the Witter Bynner Prize for Poetry from the American Academy of Arts and Letters, the National Book Critics Circle Award, the Los Angeles Times Book Award, the T. S. Eliot Prize, has been a finalist for the National Book Award, and has received numerous other grants and awards for his work. He lives in Provincetown, Massachusetts and Salt Lake City, where he teaches at the University of Utah.

Photo Credit: Ted Rosenberg